Where They Know

*To Ellen —
in friendship and
adventure in the art.
Clark*

BluesTango

ISBN: 978-0-9825684-0-8

© 2009 A.M. Clark
mexclark@hotmail.com
207-354-0051

for Lola

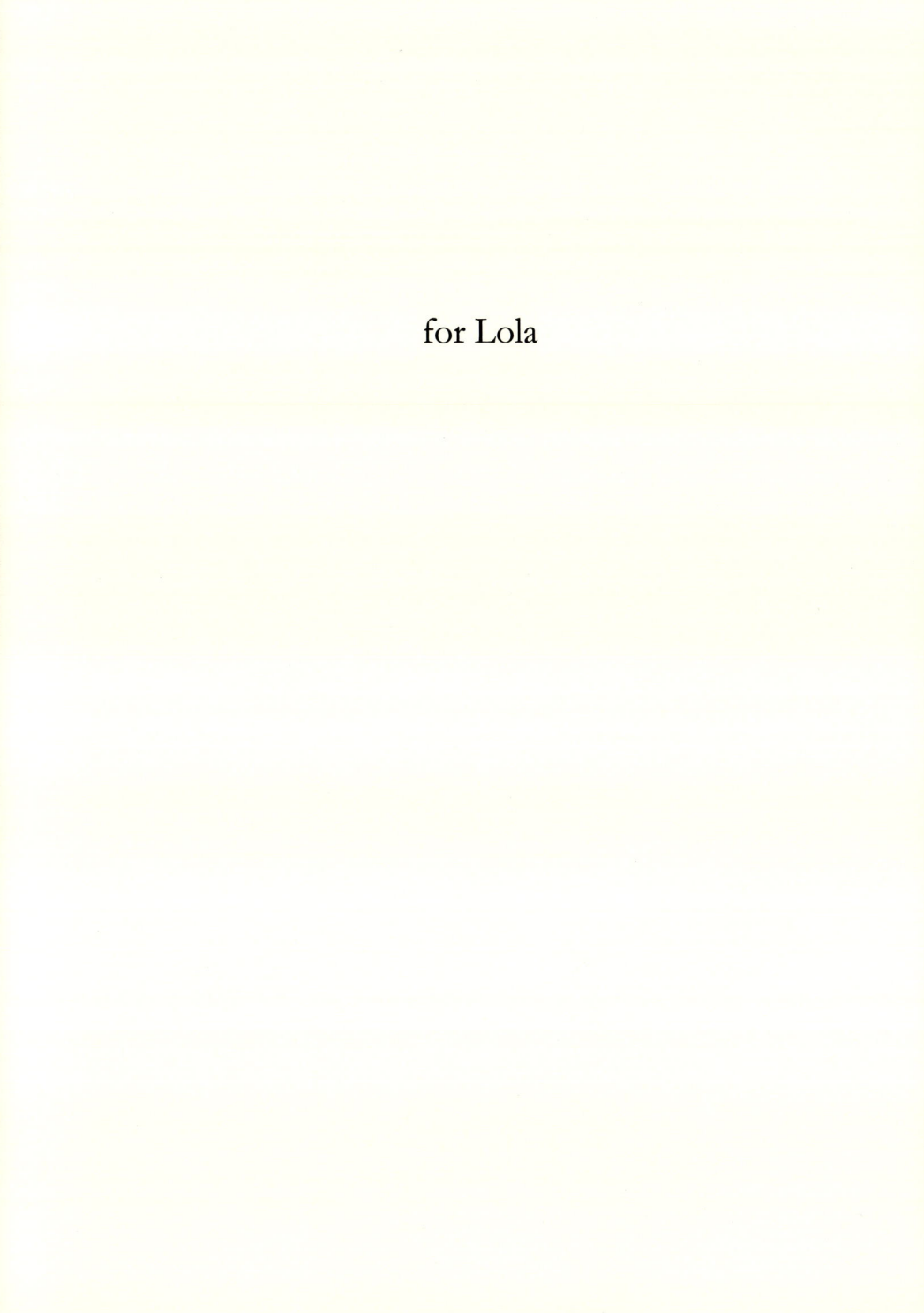

Contents

Before

Eight Loud Hounds   11
Out of Nature   12
It was a night full of kisses   13
Woman by a Pool   14
Camp   15
Inside the rain   16
Being in pleasure   17

Where They Know

Lazing on the edge   21
Poem   22
La Lengua   23
Mother of Midnight   24
Great Blue Heron   25
Sun and Ice   26
In You   27
Where They Know   28

After Midnight

On a Postcard   31
Black Coffee at Sabor   32
After Midnight   33
Late Afternoon at the Blue Parrot   34
Her Alternate Reply   35
First Poem in a New Place (The Yellow Bird)   36
Green Bowl   37
In the Park, Merida   38

Before the Next Scene

Fantasy on Absence   41
And Still No You, Morena   42
New Year's Day   43
Tinker Mack   44
A Tarot   46
Before The Next Scene   47

A Dragon Who Wakes

Painting a Picture   51

Before

Eight Loud Hounds

A young woman with eight dogs
sat in the grass and chewed gum,
observed her feet or stared ahead
to where the road had turned
beneath the full grown summer
(her hair fell long and yellow
to the green that grew to meet it)
sat and chewed and whistled softly
to the eight loud hounds who ran
in circles around my car, then
stopped to gnaw the wheels of
my intention to move along.

Out of Nature

A lion is walking toward
an antelope. Both know.
In recognition of the gravity
of what's happening, even
the wind stops its whispering.

But how did it know this time that
one of them desires an equal
to her nervous regard, to the unsuspected
speed cupped in her light hooves,
or that the other, moving quickly now,
has seen one perfect enough to flee
the exact strength of him?

There are clouds of panic, anyway,
torn from the stubborn dust of all
previous Africas. But as the roaring artery
feels the hot fulfillment of that mouth,
its blood rushes out to it
as if it were a kiss.

It was a night full of kisses and no one to kiss.

Most of the fireworks had gone off above the trees;
the rest burst behind a tangle of black branches,
making *them* more the object of our ahs.
Then clouds and rain blew in, driving us all inside.

Later, when it cleared, there was a moon, as anyone
could see, but it was the wrong one or two of us
who felt something of its power, even going down,
our smiles too fixed, our unknown sides facing away
toward those same stars the given light had hidden.

Woman by a Pool

Evening bends about
a woman by a pool,
folds upon her lying there,
cave of flesh in early
summer air.

Evening, breathing as
she breathes, stirring, as
her hand stirs the water
into blue and gold
and green.

The day has left its
sediment of hours,
musk of heat, a book
abandoned.

She's heard the tunes of ice
in tropic drinks and watched
the flickering by of
daylight things.

The lizard grass has
slipped beneath
her feet.

Camp

Here we are in yet another place,
one more half way home, this time called Camp.
It's in a good spot, a locale of beauty,
and the rent is paid, even if so late
the owner's feeling genuinely pissed,
so tells us: No, you may not use the boat
and no new oven in the stove for you.

So we say alright, it's she who has to stay
in town and sweat and pay the taxes
while we, for the sin of worldly poverty,
have all these blossoms to ourselves in league
with bees toward summer fruitfulness, a big
Moon Bay, the famous Turtle Rock and
blue-eyed grasses at our door. O, and yes,

we can unplug the phone, for "business" sake,
trash the tube away in storage, and while
the tides make constant music with the rocks,
we'll strip and love out loud on every saggy bed,
then rise and write on paper with the dream
and call it art and life and love and good.

Inside the rain

inside the roof
inside the walls
inside our skin
inside our heads
inside our thoughts
inside the heat
our hearts provide
inside the air our lungs
make personal
inside my hand
reaching to touch you
inside my desire
to be inside you
to have you
inside me
inside you
inside this rain
that keeps us
here inside

Being in pleasure,

there's only you and I
some morning hour,
pushing, pressing, piercing:
airborne darts on line
to improvised targets,
earthpoints we aim for,
trying not to try too hard.

Then coffee with the Kama Sutra:
The Clinging Vine,
Climbing The Tree,
Sesame Seeds In Rice…

Kiss the forehead, eyes, ears,
both cheeks, the lips...
Mouth Congress since we are
two beasts as well.

Your summer dress is knotted
to one side at the hip,
one full breast bare.
You have the full woman share
of wombpearls and woman semen
that rains and rains.
And the long passion.

Sometimes we can only hit the target.
There isn't any choice.

Where They Know

Lazing at the edge of a volcano,

my mind becomes the friend I thought I lost,
becomes an evening veery saying No,
I have no silver sounds except for you.
And at the ending of a summer day
creation rests from labor on itself,
sends veeries from its throat and starts to feel
the microscopic universe expand
in ease, though rocks are burning liquidly,
close beneath a tide that's coming in and
bringing what another bird will dive feet first
to catch and tear apart and not call glory,
but not unbeautiful, my mind to bless.

Poem

Another day crawling out of the fog,
the just past full moon last night, high supplicant
to the foghorn through the trees, to the air
between two houses linked again by mist
and heron calls and our love embellished eyes
in this real dream called midsummer, when stars
are always lit and sacrament is the taste
of sweat on our lover's body.

La Lengua

I'm living out your legend on my tongue
(this is the holy land we're wandering in)
with you tasting like the words that come to me,
this tongue tracking down your softest wheres,
these words tickling my throat. But in your flesh
I know what worship is, tongue directly
to the salt skin and fathoms of yourself
(not under water, in a new salt air),
word complexioned and as a long earth quake
in which the universe of you is laughing me
to go down and down to make up all the words
that will never equal you, wave and matter
as the story in the language of our dream
together: goddesses and gods of sweat,
of breasts and hands and lips that only speak
when there's nothing left to say but: Linger,
in the dark place where your thighs are met by
what of me is light enough to find you.

Mother of midnight,

                        deep inside a star,
is it you who wakes us out of sleep
so we might see, losing grace in stumbling
over roots against the dark, our dream
spread out across a cold September sky?

Does summer have a simple place somewhere
in after alls, in suns you live inside
and never die, or kiss a friend goodnight?

Or has it always been like this, a charge
of midnight questions out of soundest sleep,
with love the root we stumble on to find
waiting in the dark as leaves become cold fires
that wither into dryness as they die?

Are skies of stars the voice you send through me,
one emissary father-moon with eyes
that make you out as what you are: our life
inside the power of a star, the tree I touched
on my way to find a little light to write in?

Great Blue Heron

Of these so cold heronwaters
Elusive counterspirit
Selfsame forager
Archaic silhouette
Elegant ungainly lifestalker
Menacing greywings
To your own kind intruding
Shy featherwings
At my physical approach
Croaking longthroat
Unlikely greatwings over
Daylight waves
Nobodied image I know
Can only be you
When I hear you late at night
Dawn remade
Wading in the alive shallows
Whispery breastplumed
Carestepping
Heronshadowed
Before that deeper water
I can see

Sun and Ice

In the soft, cold quiet
of a day like today,
my heart becomes a leaf…
whichever way it blows
or doesn't blow, is near.

Outside, the cold trees warm
with sun in an icy grace
of clearness, my blood,
a sun, my eyes, like the air,
everywhere at once
but still as still in where
they stop to look.

The piled-up ice across
the cove is radiant.
There hasn't been a sound
all day but what I've heard
speaking from a new book.

The wind I'm in is you, though,
this heart, my leaf of hours
with blood that waits and
doesn't wait and waits…
your eyes a book for me
to read up close some time
the sun and ice you are.

In You,

I can see what stuff shadows are made of
and how clay can become a kind of light,
how I'm like a fish who can't not swim
into a world where the seagrass is swirling
when you lift up your arms on a hot day…
feel in you the raw green of a plant
being changed to heat in an oven of blood,
what lies not awake, not asleep inside
the shell of another day promising
all of itself to no pearl expectations…
smell in your animal, the flower of
my peacock tongue, the instant its tastes
are lavish enough by creed to taste you,
the dictionary of my senses unspelled
as kisses, and the rote freedom gathered
in the feathers of a bird who spills the wind
when her eyes behold, who can claim by law
what no one else would ever see: scales
of brief rainbows and the world's creation.

Where They Know

Your fingers, where they know where they're going,
my eyes on where they're going, my tongue on
the smooth crux of the story you allow me
sight to see, vulnerable to your own freedom,
oiled up out of yourself a silk lifetime,
teaching me who you are, everyone you are,
where the goddesses are freest with the gods
who never plan but give away desire,
like your oils, like your musks marry me
ringless as close as this, so far away,
something writing me, feeling good in my hand.

After Midnight

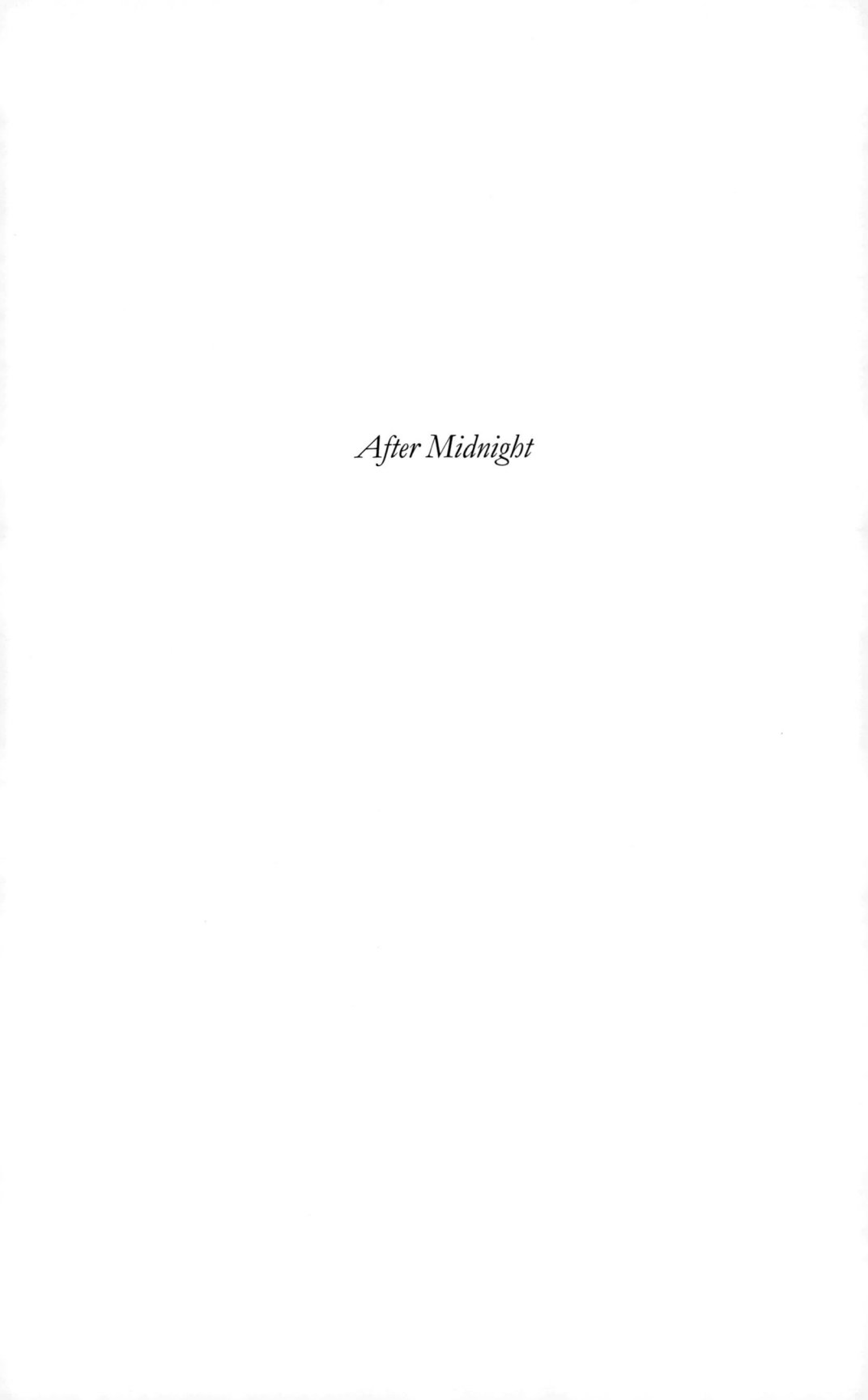

On a Postcard

Having never not left,
what is there left to say
but: Hello again, dear.
The raven's flown and lit
in his favorite trees:
inside, an old white pine,
and out, this short lived palm
down where it's just too hot
not to linger in shade
and spice his cooling drink
and round his midnight hours
with darker sounds the moon
will understand, so when,
by day, though hidden in
another kind of light
she'll know his sun-black eyes
and love his sun-black blood
as her own ruby tides.

                to Lola

Black Coffee at Sabor
> *"I'm in heaven, but is heaven in me?"*

Behind rainbow shades: what suns! peer out from
shadows onto sunstruck folks from everywhere
strolling by, "Return to Jamaica" loud
like rum honey into us from next door,
blue umbrellas under blue cotton skies.

O find me a place anywhere down here,
let me climb the slow days with this black pen,
invite all the loves not here to taste this
pleasure with me in a long heaven of sand
this morning's Coronado gleamed against:
its fast life, words of awe from all of us,
its end, our pleasure-feast ashore and away,
our new desire, its ancient life inside us
our feet will tell the story of tonight
in steps' electric measure, while skin to skin
sounds the air to God, not far from Cozumel.

After Midnight

Wind and haze and heat and thunder
from the waves that never stop but
sometimes soften under clouds to
milk their ease in softness for a while,
though cruised inside by rays and fish
the colors of a rainbow gift
no judgment minded god would give,
in love with her own pleasure.

And the days go on in wonder:
for eyes, the sights themselves they see,
for ears, the sounds they freely hear,
with touch, the sun soft lips of loving you,
Miss After Midnight on the beach last night.

Late Afternoon at the Blue Parrot

We're lolling, after all, and Pedro Juan
is right on time to ring the happy hour.
Puzzle stupor from the night before
reins in the impulse for a plunge, a swim,
a stroll beyond where others always go.

The bluest sea comes crashing at our feet.
Profound diversions amble by, baked to
tan enchantment (tied by the fewest strings)
along the cooling corridor of sand.
What was it that we really came here for?

Last night the stars were standing on their heads.
Liquid motion of a life: a sea still warm
from the burning sun, black fathomed in
to fill up footprints with a hiss, the air,
mad messenger of music, made of silk.

Lost in the moontalk of a naked hour,
we watch another day go softly by.
Ice is melting slower by a hair and birds
with scissor tails, black feather wings, soar
above the longing waters closing in.

Her Alternate Reply

But everything is what I want to be,
and so what if I turn to dust and blow
away with you today and let whole trust
leave fear and all the hallowed shoulds back in
that disappearing land of - No, señor!

Because my yeses brew like sunlight in
my darkest place, where you and I belong, señor,
and finding that I'm teeming after all
in this, invite you wholly into me,
O god I am the dust-born goddess for.

And O the holy music we will hear
together as we crumble and we burn
and taste this universe we are each time
our yeses and our yeses have their way.

First Poem in a New Place
        (The Yellow Bird)

And nothing. Windows gaping, clouds passing through.
Somewhere an engine is shredding damp air.

A yellow bird stops to gawk, then flies away
while I, strange denizen, floating tourist
lingering tongueless go on praying
to Ample God, then watch as that bird
with the hot black eye flies back again
to sway at lunch in a gentle frenzy
while another skitters songlike out of sight:
licks of sunlight pecking at a few blood drops,
upside down the moment in mild mid air.

Mind the all day sun. Douse the dry ones left, first thing.
Go swim beside what's promised to be swimming
in the wide lagoon. Forget not the love
that's winnowed you from all who've rushed to die.
Blind, the fruit gives wing. Bright, the seed is buried.

Green Bowl

My green bowl glistens with the oil
that melted down by fire two lives
of onion root and garlic bits
to kick awake a modest dish
and we'll go on living for a while.

I'd spent the whole day all alone,
pressed upright in a sunlit gale,
my heart unwoven by two threads
suspending me I spun between
(blood creature of the thinnest air)
and heard as someone made of stone
I thought, that love was very near
but not for me.

                So I borrowed
from an absent cloud or two a tear
and with an awful pull fell free
to hurry back and dream and to
consider with a knife, its edge
against which life I needed more…
but cut, thank god (and lit the oil)
the onion and the garlic bulb,
then threw in all the coldest rest.

In The Park, Merida

Drums and sirens and the hooing of doves,
a tour bus emptied, a snapping page of news,
and dozens of our interloper tongues
are torpid murmurs in the drenching shade.

Nearby, schoolgirls laugh and walk away,
not noticing the country boy in rags,
half dozing on a bench. A shoeshine man
lays out his waxes on an old blue tarp.

A homeless holy man arrives, not naked,
not down here, except his feet, as black as
the melting streets. The boy is fast asleep.

The ancient trees are whitewashed up their trunks.
It's said to keep the giants free of ants.

A gringa lopes on by, half a gypsy,
half the girl we had to leave next door.

The shoeshine man sits down to face his chair.
We both look up to watch the burning sky.
The gringa strolls on back the way she came.
There's a slight, electric scent of rain.

Before The Next Scene

Fantasy On Absence

is another night with never you,
entering my dream to lie beneath
or ride above me, your face a moon,
your hair all tangled in the ceiling stars.

Fantasy on absence is the aftermath,
the strange geometry of what is you
and never you, soft mission of your body
inside every dreaming cell of me who only
awes himself with never you in smiling
relativity.

                    My speed of light,
you square me with your energies and my
fantasy on absence is the never
ever you so ever close inside me.

And Still No You, Morena

Not that I'm in waiting anymore.
That little house where morning glories
wrapped around the broken gate, is gone.

They're all so blurry sharp, those days,
when heat would settle into dust and then
we'd walk out just to hear cicadas
where the trees grew tall, and nothing else,
to smell the smoky residue of fields
that had been burned to make them green.

The cistern dripped our afternoons away
and soft we spoke against each other's lips
and slow we took our time with all the rest
until the evening stars had gathered at
the window where a cat was smiling down.

New Year's Day

Into the present tense of Aught Aught Nine
(after strapping playful pistols to my thighs)
I woke with you (and you) again, pronounced
(unspoken, in my head): The day has come
for making perfect sense (and squirrel pie),
pronounced (unspoken, like the rest) that I
will ask you one more time if love is this
contentious lack of war we live (then draw
my pistols as you sort through photographs).
But watch, instead, your eyes and then your smile
light up (resolutions are a bust) and say:
It's New Year's Day, my love. Let's go back to bed.

Tinker Mack

One quick cast, flicker of a silver lure,
was all it took and it was all too fast
for even any stalking pleasure.
But the view was right: a brutal fog,
a barely tipping dock and deep salt tide.
Off somewhere, I heard a small child cry.

My barbed new target, fresh from cellophane,
hissed and with a plonk began to sink.
I'd snapped the bale and turned the spool but twice
when the slender rod began to quiver
(like my heart) and I knew I had one hooked.

I plucked him up (too beautiful to keep!)
abruptly on my lightweight line, tiger-
mottled green and dagger sleek, his flank
a molten silver, astonished (I saw it
in his onyx leer) to be suddenly
so gasping in such a choking air.

I held his trembling life in my left hand
and with the other eased the hook on out,
then knelt to put him gently back, alive.
The fog was cold, the water, as I knew, was ice.

I cast again and didn't have to wait,
cut the three allotted to my taste, quick
each time across the spine and quit the place

(fog now inside my head) to drive back home
where an hour exactly later I could sit
with book and chilled down glass of wine to
a long anticipated, solitary feast
of tinker mackerel broiled up crisp with
pepper, oil, shake of salt, squeeze of lime.

A Tarot

I see your Swordplay is a slight of hand
in which you disappear to come again
the self proclaiming savior of old Knaves
and Knights, someone who gives his Hearts away.

I see you see through no one else's eyes,
watch you enter rooms, go onto floors where
music spells the steps and know that you don't mind
an always starting out again the Fool

whose cliffs you tango near, still holding back
your Ace (the Hanged Man up your sleeve) and out,
your Cups in toasts to brinks you have to dare,
still blessed in all the arts of He and She.

Before The Next Scene

It may not matter that the moon was up,
but I was cold and bored and waiting
while the warmer extras sat together
in their game of what, given exile
on an island plunked in nowhere and two
choices only, they would choose to bring…
listened at the edges of their laughter
as the ring of voices circled round the fire
until it stopped with one young woman,
strange to me who, looking through the darkness
in my shadowy direction (I saw eyes
and not a smile) said: Cigarettes. And him.

A Dragon Who Wakes

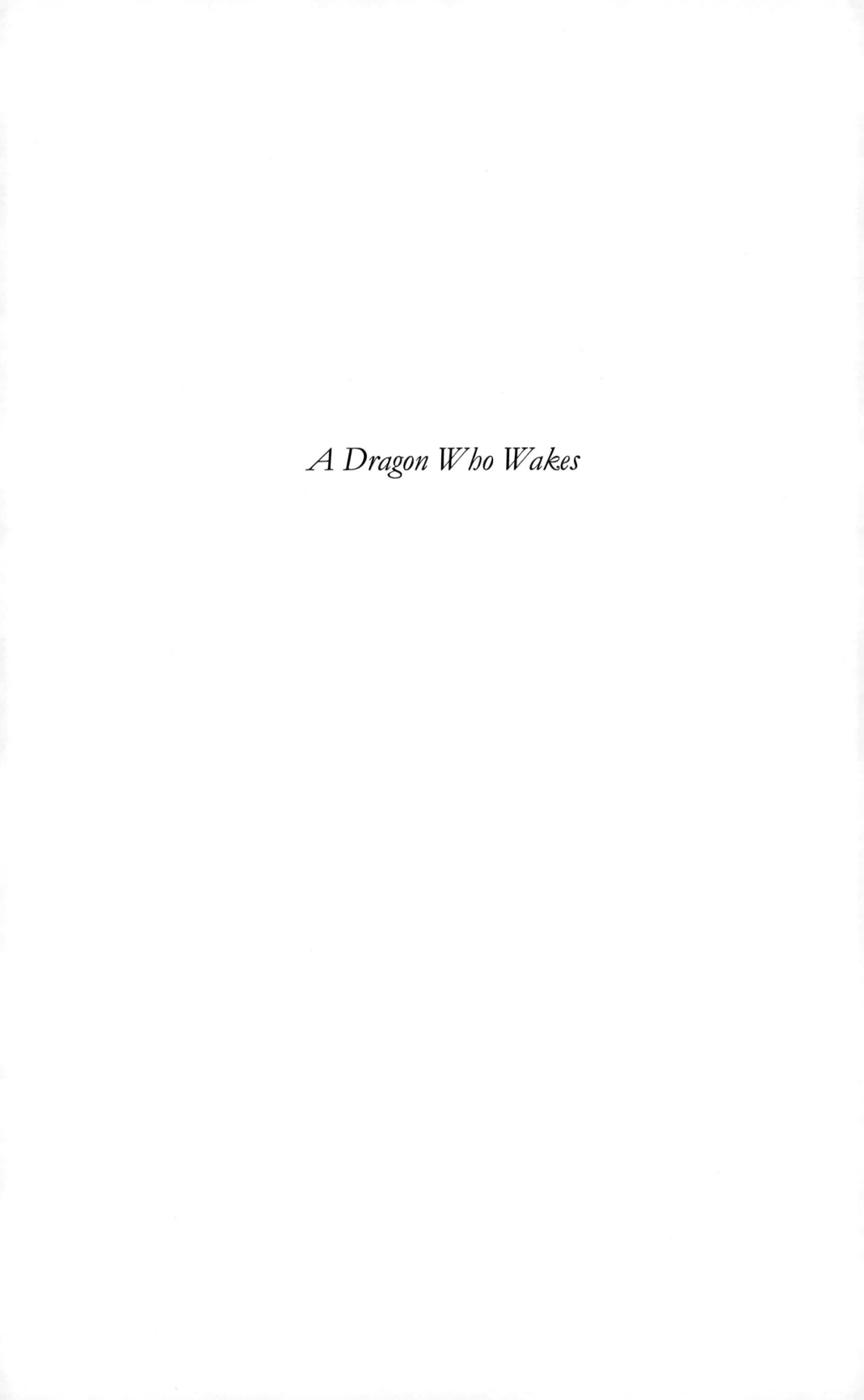

Painting a picture on paper in my lap,
making a mountain and the pathways up,
birds in the air, clouds at any level,
all the leaves in favor: green, blue, reddish
token buds, tracks and scat that just appear,
woods and rocks with eyes that haunt me freely,
trails of old shadowlands lighted by fires,
no problem even if the clouds have broken
into a ten minute deluge forever…
a hut, a palace, the quick flag of a deer,
crying-out hares, squirrels for a rag of tail,
black pools at the bottom of a held back stream
where fish numberless as stars are clamoring
to be reeled in in this fever of more and more…
rockfest galaxies not spurning my dream:
of a doorway to a white something that's
slumbering away, which was once told
as the story of a dragon who wakes on
being touched, and then the world is a place
to be seen from the back of the bird
it becomes for you to climb on and fly
anywhere at all it wants to take you.

                      For Lyonelle

The following poems appeared in:

The Caribbean Writer:

Black Coffee At Sabor, In The Park, Merida

Wolf Moon Journal:

Great Blue Heron, Tinker Mack

The Adirondack Review:

Eight Loud Hounds

Clean Sheets:

La Lengua, Where They Know